PRAIRIE GIANTS

PRAIRIE GIANTS

Compiled by Hans Dommasch

Western Producer Prairie Books
Saskatoon, Saskatchewan

Cover and book design by McKay Goettler Design
Printed and bound in Canada
Cover photograph by Myron Kozak

The publisher acknowledges the support received for this publication from
the Canada Council.

Western Producer Prairie Books is a unique publishing venture located in the middle of
western Canada and owned by a group of prairie farmers who are members of
Saskatchewan Wheat Pool. From the first book in 1954, a reprint of a serial originally
carried in the weekly newspaper *The Western Producer*, to the book before you now, the
tradition of providing enjoyable and informative reading for all Canadians is continued.

Canadian Cataloguing in Publication Data
Dommasch, Hans S. 1926–

    Prairie giants

    ISBN 0-88833-196-7

1. Grain elevators - Prairie Provinces - Pictorial
works.   I. Title.

TH4461.D65 1986   725'.36'09712   C86-098006-5

CONTENTS

PREFACE

When I first arrived on the prairies, the land imposed its overwhelming presence on me with a dazzling array of light and color as far as the eye could see. As a newcomer and as a photographer, I learned very quickly to isolate and focus in on the countless tiny wonders of nature that could be found highlighted against the vast backdrop of the land. I might marvel at a crocus or at a cactus growing in the sandy soil, or enjoy the abundance of insect life or wildlife. Gradually, I became familiar with my new surroundings.

One element of the prairie landscape that never failed to impress me was the anomalous vertical grain elevators standing out against a background dominated by horizontal lines. Their impressive size and color against the earth and sky made them excellent subjects to photograph. And photograph them I did for the next fifteen years, when, all of a sudden, these utilitarian structures took on a new meaning for me. I began to see them as skyscrapers, sentinels, monuments—prairie giants. And I made the decision to chronicle their presence on the land.

In my experiences photographing these majestic prairie giants, I have seen railroad tracks, lit by a beam of light, leading the eye to these magnificent structures embraced by the changing light of dawn or dusk. I have witnessed raging blizzards that try with all their might to obliterate everything in their path. In these tempests, sky and land fuse like passionate lovers. Road and town are hidden behind white. But the imposing outline of the elevator looms up from behind the veil of swirling snow, a steady beacon to the traveler in the surrounding chaos.

I sense a relationship between the country graveyard and the country elevator. The juxtaposition of these two powerful symbols causes me to think about the past, of a time when the greater part of men's and women's energies was channeled toward conquering the land and the elements and toward harnessing them to serve the needs of the early settlers. To me, the elevator marks the graves like a tombstone and unites the early inhabitants of the prairie communities with those who followed. It stands as a marker to the achievements of successive generations and symbolizes the continuity of life in the prairie town.

As I have witnessed the beauty and grandeur of country elevators, so have I witnessed with sadness their destruction. Miles and miles of railroad tracks have been abandoned. The lifeline of the elevators on these lines has been stolen away; they have been rendered purposeless. Some of the traditional wooden structures on active lines are being replaced by chunky concrete or metal elevators with enormous appetites for storing large quantities of grain. As each tall, slender prairie giant is pulled to the ground, in the midst of splintering wood and clouds of dust, it marks the end of an era.

To do justice to the story of *Prairie Giants*, I searched far and wide for suitable photographic images. The book before you now is the culmination of seven years' work and a rigorous selection process from the nearly four thousand images that were submitted to me by photographers in almost every province in Canada and some parts of the United States. I wish to thank all those who shared their pictorial experiences with me. I am only sorry that limited space would not allow me to include many more of the excellent images that I received.

I sincerely thank the grain companies for their contribution to this book and the many people who, in sharing with me their experiences, helped me tell the story of my emotional response to the giants of the prairies. I hope the images in this book will reveal the many facets of the country elevator, perhaps awaken old and fond memories, and provide a lasting testament to these truly magnificent prairie giants.

HANS S. DOMMASCH

INTRODUCTION
by Brock V. Silversides

Grain elevators—stark yet colorful signposts of the prairies—have become the most obvious and most admired symbol of western Canada. As the only man-made structures to make their presence felt on the endless plains, they are the one example of architecture that is instantly recognized as western and as a visual metaphor for the backbone of the prairie economy—grain farming.

The omnipresent country elevator, the skinny wooden structure erected in almost every prairie community, became such an integral part of western life that a settlement without one was an oddity. Jean Swanson eloquently describes how the country elevator almost became a part of nature itself:

> The elevators became so characteristic a feature of the landscape that the fact that they were not indigenous to it became lost in their very familiarity. Old Indians and early settlers would remember the illimitable unmarked plains. Once the elevators and telephone lines were constructed, they became as much a part of the scene as the ground-hugging crocus in spring, the courageous little poplar groves, and the immensity of the sky![1]

HISTORY

The emergence of the grain elevator in the 1880s was closely connected to early settlement of the prairie provinces. At that time there was only one source of liveli-hood for most Westerners, and that was agriculture. The crowded countries of Europe, unable to grow sufficient grain to feed themselves, started looking to the New World to provide them with wheat, one of the world's most important food staples. Prairie farmers rose to the challenge and the agriculture of the West became specialized in wheat production for export.

The first major problem was transportation. In 1876, 857 bushels of western wheat were bagged and loaded onto a steamboat, carried up the Red River to Saint Paul, Minnesota, and then shipped east by rail. For the next ten years, the physical handling of wheat remained slow and awkward. Farmers would haul grain loose or in sacks to flat warehouses along the railroad. After weighing, the precious commodity would be shoveled or lifted manually onto a rail car. It was back-breaking, slow work and the grain was moved in extremely small amounts. If a farmer lived some distance away, it might take him a week or two to fill a single car. And this was time he could ill afford to spend away from his farm at the busiest time of the growing year.

This method simply had to be made more efficient. By 1880, farmers who had previously eked out a meager existence found their farms flourishing, and the burgeoning supplies of grain provided new headaches. How could they get it all to market? Once grain buyers realized that they had to handle the product in bulk, the key to greater profits and lower handling costs became obvious. The next problem was how to store the bulk grain and then load it into a boxcar.

Originally, farmers and the railway company disagreed as to what kind of structure would be best suited for handling the flood of grain at railway sidings. Most farmers wanted a relatively small building, one that they could afford to erect themselves and that could store their crops separately until each farmer accumulated enough for a boxcar. The Canadian Pacific Railway wanted to erect a larger structure which, because of its size and design, would make the loading of grain easier, cheaper, and quicker for the railway.

The vertical type of warehouse that emerged was called a grain elevator. Although already in use in the states of Minnesota and North and South Dakota, there were few examples in the Canadian West. The first grain elevator in the prairie provinces was a rounded silolike structure built in 1879 at Niverville, Manitoba. The evolving rectangular design, which was easier to build, was introduced at Gretna, Manitoba, by the Ogilvie Milling Company in 1881.

In addition to the country elevator, known as the primary elevator, the other kind of elevator in Canada is the terminal elevator—a massive, concrete structure found at the country's major ports like Quebec City, Montreal, Thunder Bay, Churchill, and Vancouver. A few inland terminals were built on the prairies just before the First World War by the federal government. Located at Calgary, Edmonton, Lethbridge, Moose Jaw, and Saskatoon, most of them are now operated by the private sector. Because so few were built so far apart, these terminals were never embedded in the imaginations of Westerners.

The CPR, in 1881 the only western railway, was eager to haul bulk grain. Trains that had come west with settlers and their effects could be filled for the return trip east. Although it built its own terminal elevators at Fort William in 1884, the CPR could not afford to construct the number of country elevators needed to start the grain rolling. It therefore encouraged private companies to build them along its railway. The incentives included free sites for those who would erect a standard type of elevator, driven by a steam or gasoline engine, and who would use the proper machinery for elevating and cleaning grain. In addition, the railway promised that its cars would not accept grain from anybody but the elevator agent. This guarantee excluded the farmer and so, until the 1899–1900 Royal Commission on the Transportation of Grain, the railway and the grain companies enforced a monopoly.

Not surprisingly, elevators arose in great numbers alongside the railway. Occasionally, a town site determined where an elevator was to be located, but usually, an elevator determined where a town was to be established. The structures were built eight to ten miles apart to facilitate grain deliveries, which were made by horse and wagon. A farmer had to be able to make one round trip per day.

The earliest businesses to take advantage of these incentives were flour and grist mill companies such as the Ogilvie Milling Company, Lake of the Woods Milling Company, Ellison Milling and Elevator Company, and Maple Leaf Milling Company. Many independent or small companies also operated one or two elevators.

A flour company usually bought only enough wheat to supply its own mill. Other companies, however, purchased grain in large quantities to sell to eastern Canada or to export overseas. These firms prospered and expanded to line companies, operating many elevators along a rail line. The first line companies included the British American Elevator Company, the North Star Grain Company, the Canadian Elevator Company, the Paterson Grain Company, the Alberta Pacific Grain Company, the National Grain Company, and the Northern Elevator Company. It was a line company, Richardson and Sons, that moved the first shipment of grain from an elevator in Winnipeg to the Lakehead in the autumn of 1883.

The elevator companies decided to organize an association so they could compare notes and problems and set guidelines governing their relations with farmers. In July 1899, the Northwest Elevator Association was formed "for the purpose of formulating rules to govern transactions between its members in the handling and shipping of grain, with the object of reducing the expenses of handling the crop of the country to a minimum."[2] The association's name was changed in 1901 to the Northwest Grain Dealers Association and in 1940 to the Northwest Line Elevators Association, but its concerns remained the same.

At the turn of the century the number of elevators mushroomed. Prairie settlement had increased dramatically and larger areas of farmland came under the plough for the first time. The Canadian Northern Railway also encouraged the growth of line companies. In 1882, there were six elevators through the prairie provinces, but by the season of 1900–01, according to one estimate, there were 333 elevators in operation in Manitoba, as well as 88 in the Northwest Territories (Alberta and Saskatchewan), with a total capacity of 12,759,352 bushels. By 1910, there were 707 elevators in Manitoba, 1,004 in Saskatchewan, and 285 in Alberta, with a total capacity of 57,043,300 bushels.

Elevators could be built in two or three weeks at a cost of $7,000 to $12,000. (By comparison, a standard elevator with the accompanying machinery would cost $750,000 to $900,000 today.)

Because farmers were dissatisfied with the service they received from the existing grain companies, they began to form their own companies soon after the turn of the century. The Grain Growers Grain Company (later called United Grain Growers) was the first in 1906; the Saskatchewan Co-operative

Elevator Company in 1911; and the Alberta Farmers Co-operative Elevator Company in 1913. With the inauguration of the three provincial wheat pools—Alberta in 1923, Saskatchewan and Manitoba in 1924—the number of elevators constructed soared again, aided by the consolidation of the second transcontinental railway.

Elevator growth peaked in 1938 with a grand total of 5,758 licensed elevators. Then, due to consolidation and changes in the grain industry, it started its slow but steady decline. As of 1985 there were 1,956 elevators still serving farmers in the three prairie provinces. There are a number of reasons for the decline. When the Depression hit in the thirties, many families packed up and left their farms, in some cases leaving whole townships deserted. After the Second World War, increased mechanization in prairie agriculture meant higher profits and larger farms. Consequently, the number of family farms declined and migration of the rural population to the cities and larger towns continued. Many hamlets and villages became nothing more than elevator points, which were expensive for the railway companies to maintain in the face of the loss of passenger and freight business.

Another reason for the decline was that the grain-handling system was no longer efficient. Country elevators were constructed when grain was hauled by horse and wagon. The short distance from a farm to the elevator suited both farmers and elevator companies. Greatly improved roads

and larger and faster trucks for hauling the grain altered the situation. As one article explained:

> Suddenly, farmers could haul a truck load of 400 bushels of grain to elevators. They could deliver grain 20 or 25 miles with greater ease than a few miles in the old days with horse teams. They could make five or six round trips a day....In making deliveries, many farmers passed up isolated elevators to which they had hauled grain, preferring to haul to larger centres having shopping facilities, as well as beer parlours and pool rooms. [3]

The half-empty elevators were not paying their way, were costing the elevator companies salaries and fuel, and were reducing the profits of the railways. The railway companies, in turn, unofficially started to eliminate unprofitable branch lines that did not carry a minimum of 30,000 bushels per track mile, a figure they considered to be the break-even mark.

After an extremely poor growing season in 1961, which reduced grain production of the prairie provinces by half, the elevator companies stepped up their policy of centralization of elevator services. This involved abandoning the more worn out and uneconomical elevators and, in many cases, the physical relocation of elevators from potential ghost towns to larger centers to add to their storage capacity. The 1961 Mac-Pherson Royal Commission on Transportation officially recommended that railways not be forced to maintain unprofitable branch lines without subsidy. This opened the way for some abandonment, which the railways generally implemented in consultation with the elevator companies in order to cause them the least inconvenience.

A further reason for abandonment involved the buying out or merging of grain companies, a trend that began as early as the 1920s and accelerated during the 1960s and 1970s. Amalgamations and takeovers have been so commonplace that, presently, there are only six major elevator companies. For instance, the Pioneer Grain Company acquired elevators from the Goose Lake Grain Company in 1922, the Saskatchewan and Western Grain Company in 1931, the Reliance Grain Company in 1948, the Western Grain Company in 1951, the Independent Grain Company in 1953, and the Inter-Ocean Grain Company in 1972. Parrish and Heimbecker bought out the Western Canadian Flour Mills in 1940, part of the Reliance Grain Company in 1948, and the Ellison Milling Company in 1975. Cargill took over the National Grain Company in 1940. The Pools also have been players in this game. The three Pools bought all the elevators of the Federal Grain Company in 1972. Federal had already merged with the Searle Grain Company in 1967.

Reducing the number of companies hastened elevator closings. If a town had several elevators, including one owned by the Pool and one by the Federal Grain Com-

pany, it was unprofitable to maintain both after the companies merged operations in 1972, especially if one of the elevators was old and in need of repair.

The closing of even one elevator, where there had been several, sometimes meant a decline in the total amount of grain delivered to that point. Since there have not been price differences for most grains for years, farmers have tended to deliver where they get better service and more space, often playing one company against another. What is important therefore is the volume of grain an elevator can handle.

FUNCTION

In the most basic terms, the grain elevator is a receiving point for the farmers' grain, a place where it is weighed, stored briefly, and sent, via the railroad, to domestic and international markets. This is its one purpose, which its design and construction reflect.

Generally speaking (and there are many exceptions), the early grain elevator was a structure thirty-two feet square and seventy to eighty feet high. It was placed on a concrete foundation two feet thick and contained sixteen to eighteen storage bins. As wheat can weigh sixty pounds per bushel, the walls had to be extremely strong. It was of a cribbed wooden construction; the inside walls were made with two-by-four inch boards, the exterior walls with two-by-six inch boards spiked together horizontally. These could withstand tremendous pressure and, even today, remain so strong that an elevator can be moved without being dismantled.

A brief explanation of the grain transaction will illustrate how the elevator worked. First, the farmer drove his wagon or truck up the ramp on the side opposite the railway tracks. The truck was weighed before and after the grain was dumped through a grill in the floor. A quick calculation of the weight difference determined the purchase price. Robert Stead, one of Manitoba's earliest writers to use farming as subject matter for his novels, described the operation in his novel *Grain:*

> Gander drove his team up the gangway into one of the elevators. He guided his four horses with a dexterity that was an art, bringing the great load to position to an inch. This was his world. The load was weighed as it stood in the wagon; the warehouseman touched a lever; the front end of the wagon went up, the rear end down; a trap door in the back of the wagon-box was opened and the wheat rushed out in a golden stream into a hopper under the driveway. It was all over in a minute. Gander got his ticket, good for cash at the bank, and drove on. [4]

The grain was collected in a hopper tank on a lower level. Then, with the aid of an elevator or leg (a continually moving, looped belt with small cups or

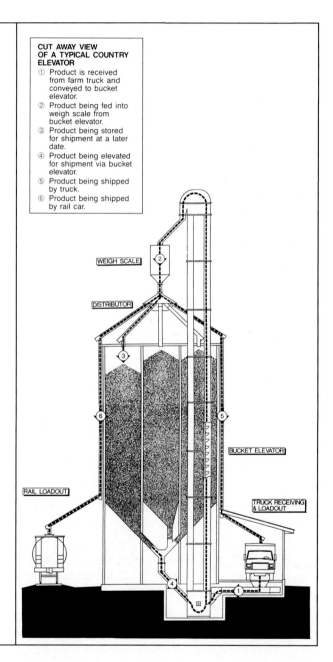

CUT AWAY VIEW OF A TYPICAL COUNTRY ELEVATOR
① Product is received from farm truck and conveyed to bucket elevator.
② Product being fed into weigh scale from bucket elevator.
③ Product being stored for shipment at a later date.
④ Product being elevated for shipment via bucket elevator.
⑤ Product being shipped by truck.
⑥ Product being shipped by rail car.

WEIGH SCALE

DISTRIBUTOR

RAIL LOADOUT

BUCKET ELEVATOR

TRUCK RECEIVING & LOADOUT

buckets attached to it), it was carried up to the tallest part of the building. Depending on the type of grain and grade, it was directed by chutes into the various storage bins. The practice of grading and separating grain bought from farmers was started by the companies in 1885, after some prodding by government inspectors. The diagram of the interior of a grain elevator (courtesy Cargill Limited) clearly shows the inner workings of a modern grain elevator.

The grain stayed in the bins until grain cars were available and then was loaded, through exterior chutes located on the track side, into grain hopper cars. There was little manual labor involved, and large quantities were moved with ease. Grain, as a product to be shipped, had an inherent advantage in that it was strikingly similar to a liquid and would fit the shape of its storage and shipping receptacles. The book *Wheat* described how it was "stored, mixed, cleaned, moved from bin to bin, and finally poured into the hold of a ship, always fluid, always in bulk, and almost without the use of hand labour." [5] The great height of the elevator facilitated the movement of grain by gravity, the cheapest form of power.

The elevator annex also functioned as an office where the agent did his paper work and a place where the elevator company sold items such as fertilizer, herbicides, seed, coal, grease, binder twine, and small implements. As well, farmers could get their seed tested for weed content and dryness.

Thus, for many years the elevator was the commercial center of a rural community.

AESTHETICS

The design of the grain elevator had nothing whatever to do with planned aesthetics or architectural beauty. It was, instead, an extremely practical and utilitarian answer to the changing needs of the grain trade. Its shape, volume, and height evolved in direct response to the demands of storing and handling grain more efficiently. As far as is known, there have been no specific names or firms connected with the design of the country grain elevator.

Elevators have attracted much attention over the years for their unique design. Initially, popular reaction was unfavorable. The traditional Canadian feelings of self-deprecation came to the fore in the earliest descriptions of the local structure. Arthur Copping in his book *The Gold Land: The True Story of British Settlers in Canada* captioned one of the illustrations of an elevator as "these helpful, if unpicturesque structures." [6] Walter Herbert, from the publicity department of the Pools, when writing about the structures in his article "Castles of the New World," expressed the view, "Every traveller crossing the Canadian prairies is impressed by the repeated sight of country elevators standing stark and rather unbeautiful at every town and siding along the railway line." He then stated that they were "a bit drab and ugly" and that "architecturally, the country elevator is nothing to inspire delight." [7]

Certainly, no Canadian architect would seriously discuss the structure, engrossed as they were with European styles. Opinions started to change when outsiders cast admiring glances and examined the elevator's origins. The famed French architect Le Corbusier became fascinated with the elevator after a visit to America in 1946. In his writings, there are few direct comments about the elevator, but a large number of indirect comments and theoretical paragraphs show his appreciation for this structure. In one chapter, he expressed the view that all architecture must respond to a specific need and that the need (in this case, the handling and storage of grain) must first manifest itself inside a structure:

> The impulse emanates from the interior and pushes against the exterior, producing various projections. This principle leads to a "pyramid like" design which can become contorted if not restrained[8]

In a sense, the elevator was an elongated and layered "pyramid" in Le Corbusier's sense of the word. Its very height and lines, however, gave it a unique prestige. He was intrigued with the concept of towers and associated tallness with dignity and value.

Perhaps what appealed most to his and other artistic minds was the elevator's utter simplicity in conception, in material, and in color. It was, in one sense, an abstraction, with the complete elimination of unnecessary decoration, standing vertical on a horizontal, flat background. Another excerpt from Le Corbusier may help to explain the feeling that there was something more than its surface appearance: "Architectural abstraction has this about it which is magnificently peculiar to itself, that while it is rooted in hard fact, it spiritualizes it."[9]

The elevator, as an example of process of architecture, was considered by Le Corbusier a "successful" building. The debate remained, however, as to whether elevators were indeed architecture in the formal sense. Many well-informed writers on the subject thought not. Alan Gowans, in his book *Looking at Architecture in Canada*, wrote that elevators were "incidental by-products of commerce, built simply as shelters to serve immediate practical needs." He went on to say:

> If we admit...that is to say "form follows function" is to define the starting-point of sound architecture, not its consummation, then it follows that these grain elevators can be no more than the potential beginnings of a distinctively Canadian architecture. [10]

Theoretical arguments are ultimately irrelevant. Companies modified the elevator to suit the needs of the grain trade. The elevator's importance was undeniable. However, the ability to modify an elevator to meet changing needs may, in the long run, cause it to become obsolete. As well as being phased out, the traditional sloped-shoulder country elevator is threatened from another quarter—elevators of a different design. Wooden elevators generally have a life expectancy of forty years, or the time needed to run through four or five million bushels of grain. Often stress from the pounding of being filled and emptied shortens that life span considerably.

Elevator companies have been considering different designs and different building materials since 1961. In that year, Saskatchewan Wheat Pool constructed the first all-steel elevator at Kenaston. Its weight was half that of the conventional wooden structure, and it was fifteen feet higher, as well as narrower. It had a flat rather than a sloping roof and the corrugated metal panels became its own structural framework. Only one other all-steel elevator was built by the Pool; the cost of construction proved to be substantially higher than that of the conventional wooden elevator.

In 1968, Alberta Wheat Pool started experimenting with precast concrete slabs for elevators and annexes. In conjunction with Edmonton engineer Nick Driedger, the Pool created a completely new design for the elevator. Called the Buffalo Sloping Bin, one observer described it as "a boxy structure that looks like a cross between a drive-in movie screen and the world's largest sloped-roof tool shed."[11] The prototype, built at McGrath, Alberta, has a vastly increased storage capacity, fills a boxcar ten times faster than a standard elevator, and needs little maintenance.

Physically and psychologically, there have been a number of reasons for the grain elevator's high profile in rural western Canada. It was, and still is, the economic center of many small towns. One of the most compelling features of an elevator is its height. The tallest building in any community commands the most attention and respect. In Europe of past centuries, the church, with its soaring spires and bell towers, was the most important structure in towns and cities. Close to home in central Canada, especially Quebec, the same idea holds true, although, of course, the veneration involved more than just the height of the building. These two qualities, height and relative importance, have always been linked, nowhere more obviously than on the prairie. O. F. G. Sitwell summed it up succinctly:

> The grain elevator was perceived as the appropriate symbol of the prairies because it was the tallest building in almost every settlement. [12]

He went on to point out that the only possible activity which could have generated enough money to enable a small town to build tall was the cultivation of grain. This is not to say that agriculture was more important than religion; rather, it was a more immediate concern. One's economic survival depended on whether one could harvest and sell a crop.

Similar to a candle in a homesteader's window at night, the elevator was also a beacon showing a traveler where food, shelter, and services could be found. Walter Herbert, the writer who saw no delight in its design, wrote, "As palm trees in the distance foretell the approach to an oasis, the Western Canadian grain elevator is always the shadow-cast-before of a village around the bend." [13] One could judge by the number of elevators the size, population, and importance of a community.

During the Second World War, young fliers, taking part in the British Commonwealth Air Training Plan, were thankful for the elevators. If they got lost, they just had to swoop down, glance at the name of the town on the elevator, locate it on their maps, and reorient themselves.

The elevator was more than just a tall building, important for the marketing of grain. There was an atmosphere, an intangible feeling, attached to it, a feeling that it was a meaningful structure in which meaningful work was being done. Even when not selling grain, farmers tended to loiter at the elevator, sensing from its operation their role in the overall scheme of prairie life. It appealed on many levels and to almost all the senses: sight, sound, touch, and smell. Again, Robert Stead writes in *Grain* about a typical small town in 1914:

> Gander drew up in the straggling street that skirted the railway track at Plainville. On his right a row of garages, livery stables, implement warehouses, grocery and hardware stores, offices; on his left the huge bulk of the grain

elevators, each with its squat little engine-room from which came the intermittent spit...spit...of the gasoline motor. The air was filled with the dust of wheat; around the elevators were drafts of chaff, in which one or two outlaw cows of the town were browsing; from the railway tracks came the sound, like rushing water, of wheat being piped into cars for shipment, first to Fort William or Port Arthur, and later to those hiving lands of Europe, now so assiduously engaged in a business of their own, but a business which could not be carried on, for long, without the help of that little red kernel, mightier than seige guns and battleships. [14]

A less appealing though no less evocative description is included in the memoirs of an ex-elevator agent:

> There is no place colder than an elevator on a January day when a wind is blowing. There are few places dirtier, when handling dusty grain and when sparrows and pigeons decide to roost there. [15]

His most powerful recollection was:

> the terrible odor of hundreds of rats. It is a wonder they did not move the elevator clean away. I have counted over 200 as they came out from under the annex on a damp morning. How I hated to go under the elevator to clean up. [16]

Regarded positively or negatively, the elevator still represented the essence of an agricultural existence. Thus, when western writers and artists became interested in local concerns, the elevator started its ascension into the realm of the symbolic. It became the most photographed and the most painted subject on the prairies. In 1950, Charles Lightbody wrote a review of Robert Hurley's paintings, describing what could be called a genre:

> What the windmill was to the painters of the Dutch School, the grain elevator is to Hurley; it is his achievement to have made many of us see it for the first time as an object of visual romance, as an expression of our feeling for our western homeland. [17]

One of the first serious artists to approach the elevator was Saskatchewan's Inglis Sheldon-Williams. An expatriate Englishman, Sheldon-Williams worked as a farm laborer and homesteader before moving into Regina to teach art. His work dealt with everyday life, rural and urban, and it is not surprising that one of his strongest works was the 1917 watercolor "Grain Elevator and Boxcars on the Prairie."

In Manitoba, it was Alexander J. Musgrove, curator and teacher at the Winnipeg Gallery and School of Art, who first turned his attention to the elevator in the second decade of this century. It is probable that he was the first artist to name a work (a 1920s watercolor of an elevator)

"The Prairie Sentinel." It was a term that gained wide usage in the years to come.

The first prairie artist to turn away from the natural landscape and concentrate solely on towns was the self-taught Saskatonian Robert Hurley, who immigrated to the West in 1923. He tried to depict, in the starkest, simplest manner, the interplay between the immensity of the prairie skies and the endless distances, and the man-made shapes of the outposts of civilization. Included in the vast majority of his oils and watercolors are an elevator (or two), telephone lines and poles, a railway track, and a colorful sky.

Some other western artists who have used images of elevators include Walter Phillips, Alfred Leighton, Cecil James, Charles W. Jeffreys, Hilda Stewart-Bell, Illingworth Kerr, and William Kurelek.

Most western Canadian photographers have produced images of grain elevators at one time in their careers. The grain companies were regular customers, and the need for picturesque scenes for tourist and board of trade promotional pamphlets was never-ending. The many who have photographed elevators include Lewis B. Foote, William J. James, Nathaniel Porter, Harry Pollard, Frederick Steele, Rusty Macdonald, and Ernest Brown.

The elevator became an exceptionally popular subject with amateur photographers and camera clubs. It offered such an imposing shape and size under a spacious prairie sky that it was relatively simple to produce an attractive image.

The popularity of the grain elevator, which noted conservationist Harold Kalman referred to as "the structure that some have called the most Canadian of architectural forms,"[18] continues to this day. Tourist posters, brochures, placemats, and postcards feature it prominently. One can buy salt and pepper shakers shaped like miniature elevators. It used to be on the Canadian dollar bill and has become one logo for a western Canadian lottery.

Members of heritage societies and the general public are becoming concerned over the elevator's disappearance. The fact that grain companies are experimenting with new structures that bear little resemblance to the country elevator gives the original a certain nostalgic aura. It is no longer considered just an efficient, roomy storage bin. Instead, many people realize that the elevator's existence is a reminder of their region's history and a symbol of their economic lifeblood.

Noted prairie architect Trevor Boddy sums up how this inanimate structure has become a symbol for a way of life:

> For poet, farmer, architect and artist alike the grain elevator is the building which is formed by and reflects back the landscape, economic wealth and social structure of the prairies. More than any other building, the wood-frame gabled grain elevator is the architectural symbol of this region. [19]

One need only try to imagine what the prairie provinces would look like if the elevators were removed to realize just how much they have become a part of the western environment and mentality.

SYMBOLS OF THE PAST

1. Built in 1879, before the tall,
    skinny, rectangular design
    became standard, this elevator at
    Niverville is believed to be the
    oldest in Manitoba.

2. Before the country elevator became a standard feature on the prairies, it was back-breaking, slow work to get the grain from early pioneer farms to market. This photograph, taken about 1899, shows a boxcar being loaded by hand.

3.   Baldur, Manitoba, prior to 1900. Grain was delivered to this steam-operated elevator in cotton or jute bags.

4. This picture of a wheat market in Wolseley, Northwest Territories (now Saskatchewan), taken in 1902, shows the importance grain elevators have always had as commercial centers in small prairie towns.

5.   Loading grain cars at St. Paul de
Metis, Alberta. The typical
elevator held 35,000 to 40,000
bushels of grain.

6. Mrs. John McEwen was the wife of one of the few private elevator operators, in Tompkins, Saskatchewan. The origin of the familiar elevator silhouette is evident in the early style of the building in this 1916 photograph.

7. Grain elevators were built eight
    to ten miles apart so farmers
    could make one round trip by
    horse and wagon per day. Bad
    weather and muddy roads often
    hampered the schedule. This
    photograph was taken at Nor-
    quay, Saskatchewan, in June 1920.

8.   In the early part of this century, large areas of land came under the plough for the first time, and prairie farms prospered. This record hauling team was photographed bringing grain to one of the elevators in Vulcan, Alberta, in 1922.

9. Farmers hauled their grain to elevators by whatever means of transportation they had on hand. Mechanized vehicles increasingly took over from horse-drawn wagons, as shown in this photograph taken in Alberta about 1925.

10. Hauling grain to elevators in
Three Hills, Alberta, around 1925.
With improved roads and larger
and faster trucks, there was no
longer any need for elevators to
be dotted across the countryside
at such close intervals, and the
railway companies began to close
unprofitable branch lines.

11. Grain elevators were efficient because there was little manual labor involved. Trucks were weighed before and after dumping their grain to determine the purchase price of their load.

12. The omnipresent country
    elevator has become a visual
    metaphor for the backbone of
    the prairie economy—grain
    farming.

13. The elevators, tallest buildings in sight, announced the prosperity and importance of the area and beckoned the traveler with services of the community, as here in Turtleford, Saskatchewan, about 1930.

14. Farmers checked their yield in the fields and agents at the elevator calculated the grade. This photograph shows a heavy crop of wheat in newly cleared land in Saskatchewan's fertile Carrot River Valley.

15. Grain was carried to the top of the elevator by conveyor belt and directed to storage bins, according to grade. In addition to storage, elevators in the 1930s such as this one in Morinville, Alberta, offered seed testing services and farm goods such as fertilizer, herbicides, and twine on site.

16. The J. H. Speers Company was founded in 1909 at 242–1st Avenue in Saskatoon as a flour, feed, and produce store as well as a grain dealership. This photograph from the 1940s shows the seed and feed supply outlet at the 238–1st Avenue location. Note the proximity of the retail outlet to the grain elevator in the background.

17. The grain piles that emerged during the fall and early winter of 1952 at Hussar were typical of many shipping points over large areas of Alberta that year. Grain production in the prairies in the years 1951 to 1953 far exceeded expectations and world markets were not calling for the volume of wheat available.

18. The sound construction of elevators permits them to be moved without being dismantled. However, the supports on this elevator shifted and it almost crashed. It was successfully uprighted and moved to its new location at Plum Coulee.

SENTINELS

SYMMETRY

SEASONS

SKYSCAPES

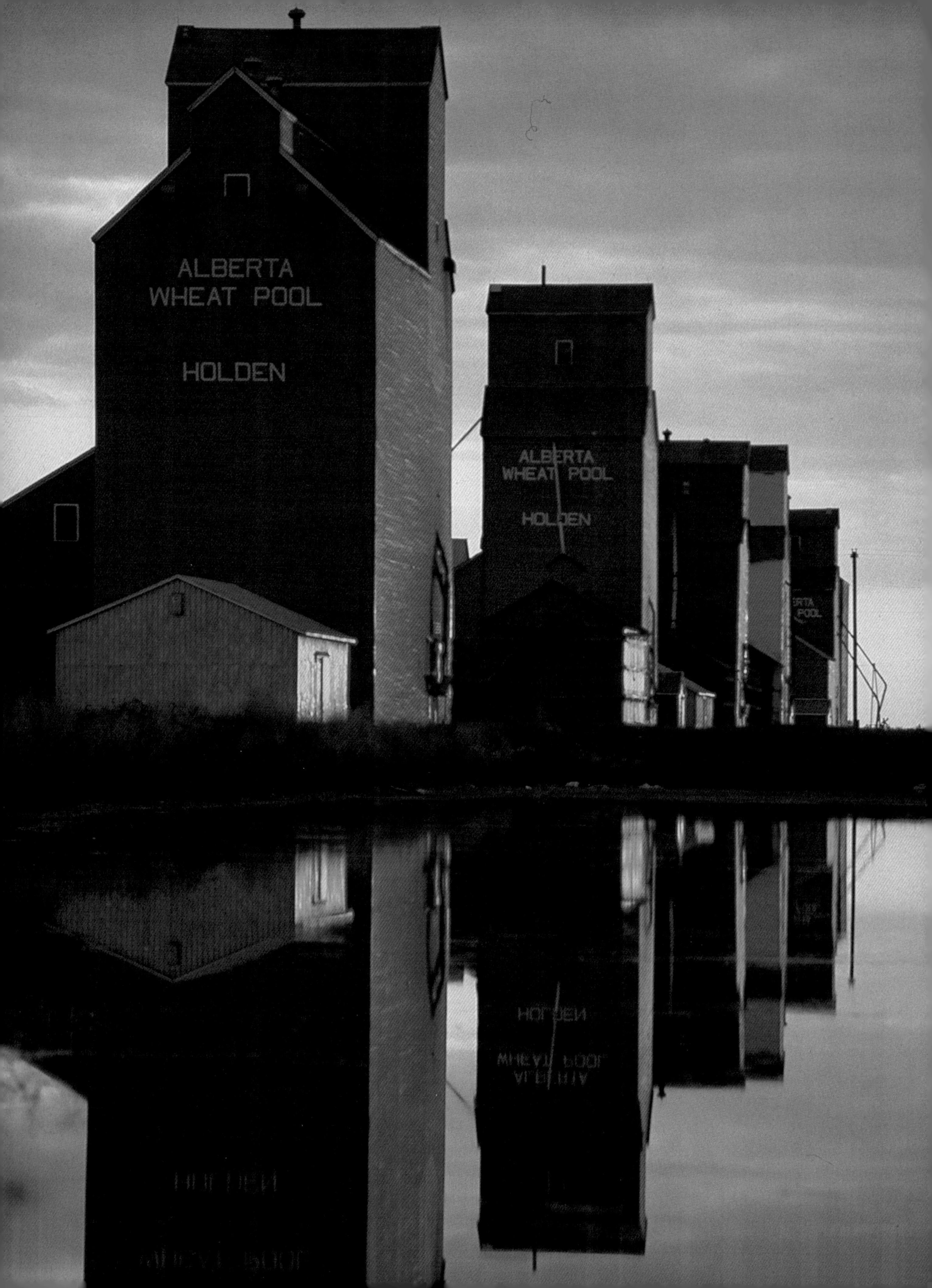
ALBERTA
WHEAT POOL
HOLDEN
ALBERTA
WHEAT POOL
HOLDEN

**CYCLES OF
LIFE**

APPENDIX

1. UNITED GRAIN GROWERS
2. PARRISH AND HEIMBECKER
3. PIONEER GRAIN COMPANY
4. N. M. PATTERSON AND SONS
5. ALBERTA WHEAT POOL
6. MANITOBA POOL ELEVATORS
7. SASKATCHEWAN WHEAT POOL
8. CARGILL GRAIN COMPANY

1. UNITED GRAIN GROWERS
Founded 1906 as Grain Growers Grain
Company
(incorporating elevators from Alberta Farmers
Co-op Elevator Company, Gillespie Grain Com-
pany, Reliance Grain Company, Midland &
Pacific Grain Corporation,[1] Canadian Con-
solidated Grain Company,[2] Canada West Grain
Company, McCabe Grain Company[3])

1. *Midland & Pacific Grain Corporation incor-*
   porated Planet Elevator Company, Midland
   Grain Company, Robin Hood Mills.
2. *Canadian Consolidated Grain Company*
   incorporated Warner Johnson Elevator
   Company, Dominion Elevator Company.
3. *McCabe Grain Company incorporated Vic-*
   toria Elevator Company, McLean Grain
   Company.

2. PARRISH & HEIMBECKER
Founded 1909
(incorporating elevators from Western Canada
Flour Mills, Reliance Grain Company,[4] Ellison
Milling & Elevator Company)

4. *Reliance Grain Company incorporated H.*
   R. Soot Grain, Matheson Lindsay Grain
   Company, Province Grain Company, North
   Star Grain Company.

3. PIONEER GRAIN COMPANY
Founded 1913
(incorporating elevators from Sterling Elevator
Company, Thorson-Olsun Grain & Lumber,
Western Grain Company,[5] Goose Lake Grain &
Lumber, Saskatchewan & Western Elevator
Company, Independent Grain Company,
Reliance Grain Company, Inter-Ocean Grain
Company[6])

5. *Western Grain Company incorporated*
   Beaver Elevator Company, Central Grain
   Company, Spencer Grain Company,
   Western Elevator Company, Mutual Grain
   Company.
6. *Inter-Ocean Grain Company incorporated*
   Congor Sanborn Company, Weyburn Flour
   Mills.

4. N. M. PATTERSON & SONS
Founded 1914
(incorporating elevators from Royal Elevator
Company, Interior Elevator Company, Western
Grain Company, Young Grain Company,
McLaughlin Ellis Company)

5. ALBERTA WHEAT POOL
Founded 1923
(incorporating elevators from Northern Grain
Company, Lake of the Woods Milling Company,
Ogilvie Flour Mills Company, Federal Grain
Company[7])

7. *Incorporated Golden West Grain Company,*
   Southern Elevator Company, Brooks
   Elevator Company, International Elevator
   Company, Maple Leaf Milling Company,
   McLaughlin Elevator Company, Western
   Grain Company, State Elevator Company,
   Stewart Grain Company, Topper Grain
   Company, Union Grain Company, Wiley
   Low & Company, Searle Grain Company,
   Alberta Pacific Grain Company.

6. MANITOBA POOL ELEVATORS
Founded 1924
(incorporating elevators from Western Canada
Flour Mills Company, Alliance Grain Company,
Reliance Grain Company, Lake of the Woods
Milling Company, Ogilvie Flour Mills Company,
Federal Grain Company)

7. SASKATCHEWAN WHEAT POOL
Founded 1924
(incorporating elevators from Province Grain
Company, Saskatchewan Co-operative Elevator
Company, Reliance Grain Company, Lake of the
Woods Milling Company, Ogilvie Flour Mills
Company, Federal Grain Company)

8. CARGILL GRAIN COMPANY
Founded 1928 (in Canada)
(entered the elevator business in Canada in
1974 by purchasing National Grain Company[8])

8. *National Grain Company incorporated*
   Atlas Elevator Company, Security Elevator
   Company, Northern Elevator Company,
   British American Company.

NOTES TO INTRODUCTION

PHOTOGRAPHIC CREDITS

1. J. Swanson, *Sky Painter: The Story of Robert Newton Hurley* (Saskatoon: Western Producer Prairie Books, 1973), p. 17.
2. C. Lamont, *Prairie Sentinels* (Winnipeg: Northwest Line Elevators Association, 1940[?]), p. 8.
3. G. Yackulic and R. Tyre, "Grain Handling...Passing of the Prairie Sentinel," *Western Business and Industry*, vol. xxxvi, no. 11 (November 1962), p. 47.
4. R. Stead, *Grain* (Toronto: McClelland & Stewart, 1926), pp. 160–61.
5. W. Swanson and P. C. Armstrong, *Wheat* (Toronto: Macmillan Company, 1930), p. 100.
6. A. Copping, *The Golden Land: The True Story of British Settlers in Canada* (Toronto: Musson Book Company Ltd., 1911), p. 49.
7. W. Herbert, "Castles of the New World," *Canadian Geographical Journal*, vol. VL, no. 5 (May 1933), p. 243.
8. J. Guiton, ed., *The Ideas of Le Corbusier on Architecture and Town Planning* (New York: George Braziller, 1981), p. 49.
9. Le Corbusier, *Towards a New Architecture* (London: The Architectural Press, 1965), p. 45.
10. A. Gowans, *Looking at Architecture in Canada* (Toronto: Oxford University Press, 1958), p. 217.
11. W. Skene, "Transformation of a Prairie Icon," *Macleans* (January 1979), p. 17.
12. O. F. G. Sitwell, "Why Did the Grain Elevator Become the Chief Symbol of the Canadian Prairies?" *Albertan Geographer*, no. XVI (1980), p. 7.
13. W. Herbert, "Castles of the New World," *Canadian Geographical Journal*, vol. VI, no. 5 (May 1933), p. 243.
14. R. Stead, *Grain* (Toronto: McClelland & Stewart, 1926), p. 158.
15. J. Bouey and M. Charlton, "34 Years an Elevator Agent," *Folklore* (Autumn 1984), p. 17.
16. *Ibid.*, p. 17.
17. C. Lightbody, "Grain Elevators and Wheat Sheaves," *Canadian Art*, vol. III, no. 2 (1950–51), p. 68.
18. H. Kalman, "This Elevator is Coming Down," *Canadian Heritage*, vol. X, no. 1 (February/March 1984), p. 19.
19. T. Boddy, ed., "Prairie Architecture," *Prairie Forum*, vol. V, no. 2 (Fall 1980), p. 134.

13 Glenbow Archives
14 Manitoba Archives
15 B. Silversides Collection
16 *Manitoba Co-operator*
17 Saskatchewan Archives Board, R–B–2969
18 Canadian National Archives
19 Mrs. Emma Carlson
20 Saskatchewan Archives Board, RA 2260
21 W. J. Oliver, Glenbow Archives, ND–8–277
22 Provincial Archives of Alberta, P 658
23 W. J. Oliver, Provincial Archives of Alberta, A 4599
24 W. J. Oliver, Glenbow Archives, ND–8–234
25 H. Pollard Provincial Archives of Alberta, P 659
26 Canadian National Archives, B–1000
27 Canadian National Archives
28 Canadian National Archives
29 L. A. Hillyard Collection, Local History Room, Saskatoon Public Library
30 Alberta Wheat Pool Archives
31 *Manitoba Co-operator*

33 Walsh, Sask., Simmone M. Flynn
34 Innisfail, Alta., Dr. Gerald Meding
35 Hague, Sask., Hans Dommasch
36 Osler, Sask., Marlee Wilson
37 Tuxford, Sask., Hans Dommasch
38 Kayville, Sask., Hans Dommasch
39 Krydor, Sask., Hans Dommasch
40 Eyebrow, Sask., Menno Fieguth
41 Carstairs, Alta., Sig Bradshaw
42 Davidson, Sask., Hans Dommasch
44 Rosthern, Sask., Zach Hauser
45 Pambrun, Sask., Telfer Wegg
46 Rock Glen, Sask., Gerry Savage
47 Ernfold, Sask., Hans Dommasch
48 Beynon, Alta., Egon Bork
49 Drumheller, Alta., Egon Bork

51	Maidstone, Sask., Egon Bork
52	High River, Alta., Connie Boyar
53	White Fox, Sask., Dennis Chamberlain
54	Muenster, Sask., Michael Brauer
55	Edgeley, Sask., R. H. Macdonald
56	Springwater, Sask., Hans Dommasch
57	Delisle, Sask., Hans Dommasch
58	Eldersley, Sask., Saskatchewan Wheat Pool
59	Weyburn, Sask., Hans Dommasch
60	Eatonia, Sask., Zach Hauser
61	Biggar, Sask., Menno Fieguth
62	Conquest, Sask., Hans Dommasch
63	Radisson, Sask., Hans Dommasch
64	Moose Jaw, Sask., Hans Dommasch
65	Kinistino, Sask., Bruce Axelson
66	Neville, Sask., Telfer Wegg
69	Elcott, Sask., Stewart Klyne
70	Hamlin, Sask., Hans Dommasch
71	Dunphy, Alta., Sig Bradshaw
72	Holmfield, Man., Charles W. Bohi
73	Gilbert Plains, Man., John Everitt
74	Maidstone, Sask., Egon Bork
75	Court, Sask., Nels A. Yalte
76	Bradwardine, Man., John Everitt
77	Maidstone, Sask., Menno Fieguth
78	Prince Albert, Sask., Hans Dommasch
80	Lyalta, Alta., Dale H. Walsh
81	Rowley, Alta., Charles W. Bohi
82	Carbon, Alta., Cameron Ertman
83	Queenstown, Alta., Dale H. Walsh
85	Melfort, Sask., Duane McCartney
86	Morden, Man., John Jacquemain

88	Osler, Sask., Wayne Shiels, Four Winds Prairie Photography
89	Rosetown, Sask., Clifford A. Crickett
90	Harris, Sask., Zach Hauser
91	Tessier, Sask., Hans Dommasch
92	Lyalta, Alta., Dale H. Walsh
93	Meacham, Sask., Myron Kozak
94	Stavely, Alta., Grace Norgard
96	Holden, Alta., Andrew W. F. Metten
97	Delacour, Alta., Dale. H. Walsh
98	Sovereign, Sask., Paul Craig
100	Foremost, Alta., Telfer Wegg
102	Saskatoon, Sask., Hans Dommasch
103	Pleasant Valley, Sask., Duane McCartney
104	Rycroft, Alta., Dave Reede
105	Regina, Sask., Kim Strange
107	Granum, Alta., Deidre Williams
108	Saskatchewan Wheat Pool
109	Saskatchewan Wheat Pool
110	Shannon, Alta., Egon Bork
111	Court, Sask., Nels A. Yalte
112	Henry Poegal
113	Henry Poegal
114	Saskatoon, Sask., Hans Dommasch
115	Saskatchewan Wheat Pool
116	Granum, Alta., Deidre Williams
118	Krydor, Sask., Hans Dommasch
119	Dodsland, Sask., Hans Dommasch
120	R. H. Macdonald
121	Edmonton, Alta., Pat Rafferty
122	Claresholm, Alta., Grace Norgard
123	Lyalta, Alta., Dale H. Walsh